Learn to Learn Again:

Effectively Use New AI Tools to Multiply Your Efficiency

By Yibing Li

© Copyright 2024

All rights reserved. No part of this book may be reproduced, distributed, or transmitted in any form or by any means, including photocopying, recording, or other electronic or mechanical methods, without the prior written permission of the author, except in the case of brief quotations embodied in critical reviews and certain other noncommercial uses permitted by copyright law.

Prologue: Learning Concepts in the AI Era — Penetration
5

Chapter 1: How to Master a Subject Area Using the Penetration Learning Method
12

Chapter 2: How to Use AI to Accelerate Your Learning
26

Chapter 3: How to Obtain Your Own Knowledge System
42

Chapter 4: Deep Replication: How to First Quickly Understand 70%
51

Chapter 5: Deep Sprint - How to Learn Thoroughly in Five Days
58

Chapter 6: How to Improve Through Deliberate Practice
66

Chapter 7: Penetrative Reading: How to Read a Book Thoroughly
79

Chapter 8: Penetrative Technology - How to Master a Technical Tool
96

Chapter 9: Penetrative Questioning - How to Master Questioning Skills in the AI Era
110

Chapter 10: Writing a Personal Knowledge Guide to Enhance Cognition
132

Chapter 11: Using the Absorption Framework to Build Your Cognitive System
145

Afterword: Everyone Can Become a Learning Expert
156

References
158

Prologue: Learning Concepts in the AI Era—Penetration

We're in the midst of a learning revolution that's as transformative as the invention of the Gutenberg printing press. Before the printing press, knowledge was limited to a select few, and learning required painstaking manual transcription. The advent of printed books democratized access to knowledge. Now, AI, particularly generative AI, is transforming learning by "putting knowledge at our fingertips."

We're at a pivotal moment where learning is set to change fundamentally. Skills and knowledge that once took years to master can now be acquired much more quickly. Moreover, certain skills will become increasingly important—like the ability to learn continuously, make informed decisions, and effectively use new tools.

In the future, people will likely fall into two categories: those who can harness AI and those who cannot. In learning contexts, this translates into those who master AI-driven methods and those who don't. This division happens gradually: some underestimate new technologies like AI, while others embrace them; some fear AI, while others are eager to learn; some misuse it, while others integrate it effectively into their work and studies. Some even become creators of AI technology and applications through learning, surpassing others. As you can see, these divisions are closely tied to learning.

The penetration learning method emerged from our experience with the "information explosion" of the internet era. The overwhelming flood of information left us unsure about mastering and applying what we learned. To tackle this challenge, we focused on developing a knowledge system between input and output—a structured approach aimed at short-term, concentrated, and thorough learning.

Facing the AI revolution, we initially felt overwhelmed by the explosion of related information. Naturally, we applied our penetration learning method to cope. We quickly discovered that this method is equally effective in addressing the "knowledge explosion" brought by AI. This stems from the concept of "penetration":

truly mastering, understanding, and applying knowledge. Adhering to this concept means thoroughly mastering even small topics, boosting our confidence in learning. Consequently, we now have the courage to tackle many new knowledge areas introduced by AI.

Of course, facing the knowledge explosion brought by AI and the ongoing new learning revolution requires iterating on our methods. Our latest exploration has crystallized into the new version introduced in this book. We considered four elements, three scenarios, and dozens of specific methods to address one key question: How should we learn if AI's knowledge and skills become ten times more powerful in the future?

In the AI era, we need to ask ourselves critical questions: What can AI do? What can't it do? Correspondingly, what should we focus on?

Navigating the Learning Landscape: Key Principles

In our rapidly evolving world, we need to rethink our approach to learning. Let's break down some common challenges and solutions:

Compass > Map

While detailed knowledge maps are valuable, the AI era demands a shift in focus. Having a compass —a sense of direction—is now far more crucial than possessing a detailed map.

Why Direction Trumps Detail:
1. With clear direction, AI can explore multiple paths efficiently.
2. Without direction, we struggle to guide AI effectively.
3. Direction enables us to critically evaluate AI's responses.

The compass of knowledge comprises judgment, discernment, and appreciation—skills far more crucial than memorizing specific facts.

Hedgehog > Fox

An ancient Greek proverb states, "The fox knows many things, but the hedgehog knows one big thing." In the AI era, this wisdom is more relevant than ever.

Challenges of Specialization:

- Information overload tempts us to explore numerous subjects superficially.
- AI's assistance makes it seem feasible to learn multiple disciplines easily.
- Maintaining focus on core pursuits becomes increasingly difficult.

The solution lies in effective learning concepts and resilience: commit to mastering each topic thoroughly.

Evolving Talent Shapes:
- T-shaped: Broad knowledge, deep expertise in one area
- ∏-shaped: Deep expertise in at least two areas
- Avoid becoming "comb-shaped" with shallow knowledge across many fields

Apple Tree > Apple

While many learners focus on immediately applicable skills(the apples), the penetration learning method emphasizes the importance of acquiring robust knowledge frameworks(the apple tree).

Benefits of Knowledge Frameworks:

1. Provide long-term value (like planting an apple tree)
2. Guide the application of knowledge and skills
3. Enable effective task breakdown and evaluation
4. Facilitate teaching frameworks to AI for execution

In the AI era, mastering knowledge frameworks becomes even more critical. It allows us to effectively delegate tasks to AI while maintaining control and understanding of the process.

By focusing on these principles—prioritizing direction, depth, and frameworks—learners can navigate the AI era more effectively, complementing AI capabilities with uniquely human skills and insights.

Part 1 How to Learn in the Era of AI

Chapter 1: How to Master a Subject Area Using the Penetration Learning Method

Learning is undergoing continuous dramatic changes, and we need new learning methods to keep pace.

What problems trouble you in learning? Many believe the issue is having too much to learn, and the solution is to squeeze out more time for studying. As a result, we, as learners, become exhausted. Some think the problem is a lack of learning resources, and the solution is to find better school courses and online courses. In fact, we have easier access to high-quality courses than ever before. Others believe the problem is a lack of learning techniques, and the solution is to master more techniques. However, these learning techniques are often difficult to transform into tangible learning abilities and outcomes.

In reality, what truly troubles us in learning is the inability to genuinely master the knowledge we've acquired and confidently apply it. As knowledge and information increase exponentially, we learn more but understand less, resulting in low confidence in our own expertise.

Faced with this situation, a viable solution is to truly master every topic you are determined to learn, whether it's new knowledge, a new tool, or a new skill.

So, how can we achieve true mastery? The process of learning a subject area moves from knowledge input to knowledge system, and then to knowledge output. Many learners focus on knowledge input and output but neglect the real breakthrough point: the knowledge system.

By setting the goal of mastering a subject area's knowledge system and using it to guide the entire learning process, we can learn and practice more effectively. With a knowledge system, we can organize the knowledge points we've learned in an orderly manner, allowing us to supplement new knowledge points when needed. You'll find that in practice, it's the knowledge system that guides you, not individual knowledge points.

"Knowing" doesn't mean "being able to do." The penetration learning method, as a set of structured learning techniques, enables learners to better acquire a subject area's knowledge system. "Structured" means these learning methods usually have a unified approach and clear steps, making it easy for you to apply them to your own learning journey.

These methods include:
1. The Feynman Blank Notebook Method
2. Deep Replication in Five Steps
3. Sprint Learning Method
4. Sprint Reading Method
5. Learning Technical Tools
6. Learning Questioning Skills
7. Writing Personal Knowledge Guides

Throughout the learning process, these methods can help you transform external knowledge systems into your own.

In addition to focusing on the knowledge system and providing structured learning methods, the penetration learning method has another important feature: it particularly emphasizes the use of technological tools in learning.

Today, our learning content no longer only includes traditional knowledge and skills. Learning to use technological tools (such as programming, professional software, and specialized equipment) has become one of the three main components of learning content. At the same time, much of the knowledge and skills we need to learn are related to new technological tools.

More importantly, technological tools have a significant impact on our learning effectiveness. The penetration learning method believes that using new technological tools well can improve learning effectiveness by more than tenfold. While there are many traditional learning methods based on experience and new learning methods based on cognitive science, the penetration learning method not only draws on a large number of experiential methods and applies views and methods from cognitive science but also particularly emphasizes new technological tools.

Artificial Intelligence (AI) is reshaping classrooms worldwide and changing everyone's learning methods. We even believe that if cleverly applied in appropriate contexts, in the most optimistic scenario, generative AI could bring a hundredfold increase in learning effectiveness.

The Origin and Impact of Generative AI on Learning

The concept of AI dates back to 1950 when Alan Turing posed the question: "Can machines think like humans?" AI has evolved rapidly over the past decade, with OpenAI's release of ChatGPT in 2022 marking a pivotal moment in its impact on individual learning.

The Evolution of AI in Learning

Before 2022, we relied on teachers, classmates, search engines, or social media for answers. Post-2022, AI chatbots like ChatGPT have become viable alternatives. This shift is powered by Large Language Models, capable of understanding and responding to human language with increasing accuracy and effectiveness.

Key milestones in AI development include:
- 2012: Emergence of deep learning, leading to breakthroughs in machine translation, speech recognition, and image processing.

- 2016: AlphaGo defeats the world champion in Go, showcasing the power of reinforcement learning.
- 2017: Introduction of the Transformer architecture, revolutionizing language understanding and generation.
- Late 2022: Launch of ChatGPT, reaching 100 million monthly active users within two months.

The Impact on Learning

Generative AI offers several advantages for learning:
1. Personalized tutoring: AI can provide instant, specific answers to various questions, potentially improving learning efficiency.
2. Reduced learning resistance: AI makes it easier to obtain knowledge, allowing learners to focus on topics requiring in-depth study.
3. Addressing the "burden of knowledge": As human knowledge expands, AI can help manage the increasing volume of information to learn.

The Learning Paradox and AI's Potential

Despite increasingly powerful learning tools, we often feel we're falling behind in keeping up with new knowledge. AI presents a unique solution to this paradox. Unlike past tools that merely helped manage the knowledge burden, AI has "no burden of knowledge" itself. Trained on vast amounts of human knowledge, AI can efficiently integrate, reorganize, and invoke this information.

Learners who effectively use AI tools may potentially learn 10 to 100 times faster than those using traditional methods. For example, in programming, AI can assist in writing code and debugging, significantly speeding up the process.

The Importance of Knowledge Systems

While AI can accelerate learning, it's crucial to note that having a strong personal knowledge system in a subject area is still vital. A well-developed knowledge system allows you to leverage AI more effectively, solving problems much faster than relying on AI alone. Without this foundation, AI's assistance may be limited or even misleading.

In the next chapter, we'll explore how to use AI to accelerate learning. For now, it's essential to recognize the transformative potential of AI in education while understanding the continued importance of developing robust personal knowledge systems.

Knowledge System: Planting a Tree of Knowledge

The term "knowledge system" can have different meanings depending on the context. It might refer to all human knowledge, with large libraries serving as tangible representations of this vast system. Alternatively, it could denote the knowledge system of a specific discipline, such as the mathematics curriculum from elementary school through university. It may also encompass an individual's entire knowledge base, including everything learned through formal education, work experience, and personal interests.

In this book, however, a "knowledge system" refers to the knowledge framework of a single topic or specialized field. This definition includes two key components: the specialized field and the knowledge framework. When discussing knowledge systems, we are implicitly referring to "a system about a particular topic or field." The optimal form of a knowledge system is a hierarchical outline, which we also call a knowledge outline.

While we use the term "knowledge system" to anchor learning content to an easily definable noun, it is essential to make this concept more concrete. To facilitate understanding, we can utilize the DIKW classification framework: Data represents unprocessed raw material; Information is processed data; Knowledge is analyzed and summarized information; and Wisdom is the insight into and application of knowledge.

The knowledge of each subject area can be organized into a tree-like structure. From bottom to top, information is summarized into specific knowledge points, which are then organized into larger points to form a comprehensive knowledge framework. This framework typically implies core concepts and principles that we refer to as the "knowledge core" of the subject.

Practical learners focus on the "knowledge framework" aspect of this structure, which includes major knowledge points and their interrelationships. By mastering these elements, learners discover how to effectively apply each core concept and principle in practice. Excellent teachers strive to clarify this part within limited course time by outlining the knowledge structure for their students. However, teachers can only present external knowledge frameworks; it is ultimately each learner's responsibility to transform this external knowledge into their own understanding. The various methods of penetrative learning aim to assist learners in quickly and efficiently making this transformation.

If we visualize the knowledge of a subject area as a large tree, individual leaves represent specific knowledge points—vast in number and easily accessible. The fruits on the tree symbolize directly applicable practical knowledge points that purpose-driven learners quickly pick and consume. The trunk signifies the main knowledge framework of the subject, while the main branches extending from it represent the frameworks of sub-topics. The hidden root system serves as the foundational knowledge that supports the entire tree; deeper roots lead to greater stability.

Strictly speaking, the knowledge system encompasses all parts of the tree—from leaves to roots—while the knowledge framework includes only the trunk and main branches. After understanding this subtle distinction between a knowledge system and a knowledge framework, we will not differentiate between them further; when referring to the knowledge system, we will usually mean only the trunk and main branches.

Using this tree metaphor allows us to vividly set our learning goal as deeply understanding the trunk and main branches—the knowledge system of the subject—helping us absorb, integrate, and apply what we learn more systematically. Once we master the knowledge system, we can use learning tools to acquire specific knowledge points more quickly and easily.

Focusing on the trunk and main branches is an effective learning strategy. Once you've mastered the knowledge system, you can confidently apply your understanding within that subject area. Throughout this book's exploration of penetrative learning methods, you will find that the knowledge system plays a central role in your learning process.

Mastering Real Knowledge, Not "Chauffeur Knowledge"

Investor Charlie Munger used to share a story that illustrates the difference between real knowledge and "chauffeur knowledge." While its authenticity is not crucial, the lesson it imparts is valuable.

In 1918, Max Planck won the Nobel Prize in Physics for his work on quantum mechanics. Despite its complexity, the subject became popular, and Planck was invited to lecture across German cities. His chauffeur, having heard the lecture countless times, memorized it and proposed an intriguing idea: he would deliver the lecture in Munich while Planck sat in the audience wearing the chauffeur's cap.

The chauffeur's delivery in Munich was flawless, even impressing the audience more than Planck's usual presentation. However, when a physics professor asked a challenging question, the chauffeur cleverly deflected, saying, "I'm surprised that in such an advanced city as Munich, someone would ask such a basic question! My chauffeur can answer this question, so I'll let him respond now."

This anecdote highlights the distinction between Planck knowledge—deep understanding gained through extensive study and practice—and chauffeur knowledge—superficial familiarity that mimics expertise. Munger advises, "When facing a problem in life, try to give responsibility to those with Planck knowledge, and stay away from those who only have chauffeur knowledge."

Interestingly, the chauffeur demonstrated wisdom by recognizing the limits of his knowledge and deferring to Planck when necessary. In our era of information overload, it's crucial to acknowledge what we don't know rather than pretending to have expertise we lack.

Key Points of This Chapter:
1. The penetration learning method focuses on mastering knowledge systems, enabling thorough learning of a topic in a concentrated period.
2. This method emphasizes the use of new technological tools to significantly enhance learning efficiency.

3. True penetration involves developing high-level cognition, including intuitive and rational judgment, appreciation, and learning confidence.

Practical Exercises:
1. Identify five new topics you urgently need to learn.
2. For a topic you believe you've mastered, assess whether you truly understand its knowledge system and have developed high-level cognition.
3. For a familiar topic, attempt to sketch its knowledge system and explain it to others.

Chapter 2: How to Use AI to Accelerate Your Learning

"To me, the computer is one of the most remarkable tools we've ever created. It's like a bicycle for the mind." This insightful comparison comes from Apple founder Steve Jobs in a 1990 TV interview. The bicycle metaphor is apt: the brain must exert effort for both you and it to progress together.

Humans have now created another remarkable technological tool—generative AI. It's rapidly integrating into our learning, work, and daily life through chatbots, smart assistants, and more. Generative AI can be considered another bicycle for thinking, expanding our cognitive capabilities.

The ability to create tools distinguishes humans from other primates. Throughout history, we've developed numerous tools for thinking: paper and pen, printed books, abacuses, and calculators. With the advent of the internet, new technological tools for thinking continued to emerge. Search engines and social networks, which can be viewed as collective human intelligence, have had profound influences. Note-taking software, often called a "second brain" for personal memory, has also become essential. Now, generative AI has joined this lineup, becoming one of the most powerful learning tools to date.

In terms of learning, generative AI has made many people feel directly challenged. Knowledge and skills that once required significant time and effort to acquire can now be accessed instantly by querying AI. While the future of instant knowledge access hasn't fully arrived, the current shock we're experiencing presents an opportunity. It prompts us to ask: How can we better leverage various new technological tools, including AI, to enhance our learning?

The 10X Principle: Using New Technological Tools to Improve Learning Efficiency Tenfold

For every new technology, there are optimists who focus on its strengths and possibilities, and pessimists who concentrate on potential risks. Our approach should be:

1. Emphasize learning and mastering new technological tools, understanding their usage tips and applying them in practice.
2. Recognize that new technological tools have shifted the focus of learning from "memorization" to "knowing how to query".

A Concise Guide to Using Generative AI: You Ask, It Answers

One of the great advantages of AI tools is their accessibility—if you can write or speak, you can use them. They understand natural language and primarily respond in ordinary text.

Think of using AI for learning as consulting a knowledgeable, smart teaching assistant. However, remember that it's just an assistant, not a teacher. Teachers possess deeper, more accurate knowledge; AI assistants are enthusiastic helpers, but their answers may not always be entirely correct. As AI technology improves, these "assistants" might eventually approach the level of teachers.

AI tools are straightforward to use: you ask, it answers. These AIs are primarily large language models that support conversational interactions with users. The words we use to query AI are called "prompts." Through the keywords in our prompts, we trigger responses from the AI. These models can understand our prompts, answer our questions, or complete requested tasks.

AI large language models possess not only text understanding and generation capabilities, but also multilingual abilities, logical reasoning skills, and a broad base of knowledge. In the following sections, we'll explore practical examples to give you an intuitive understanding of how to leverage AI in your learning journey.

Prompt:
How can people use AI tools in varieties of way in order to help them study more efficiently? Use simple language so that a third grader would understand.

Answer:
Here's a simple explanation of how people can use AI tools to study more efficiently, written for a third grader: How to Use AI Tools to Study Better

AI tools are like smart helpers that can make studying easier and more fun! Here are some ways you can use them:

1. **Homework Help**: *If you're stuck on a math problem or a question, you can use an AI tool to get help. Just type in your question, and the AI will show you how to solve it step by step. It's like having a teacher right there with you!*
2. **Writing Assistance**: *When you have to write a story or a report, AI can help you make it better. It can check your spelling and grammar, and even suggest new words to use. This way, your writing will be clear and exciting!*
3. **Study Planning**: *AI tools can help you organize your study time. They can remind you when to study for a test or when to do your homework. This helps you stay on track and not forget important things!*
4. **Practice Tests**: *You can use AI to create fun quizzes or flashcards. This way, you can practice what you've learned and get ready for your tests. It's a great way to make sure you remember everything!*

5. ***Finding Information****: If you need to learn about something new, AI can help you find information quickly. It can search the internet and give you answers, so you don't have to spend a lot of time looking.*

Using these AI tools can help you study smarter, understand your lessons better, and even make learning more fun! This explanation uses simple language and relatable examples to help a third grader understand how AI tools can assist them in their studies. If you need any changes or more information, feel free to ask!

How to Use AI to Enhance Learning Effectiveness by 10 Times

Learning is the process of transforming external knowledge into one's own. We can view this process from two perspectives: cognitive (understanding input knowledge) and action-based (applying learned knowledge). Both cognition and action can be divided into three parts:
1. Eliminating obstacles
2. Deepening understanding
3. Accelerating output

AI can significantly improve our learning effectiveness in each of these aspects. Currently, AI is already performing well in various learning scenarios, and its effectiveness continues to improve.

Using AI to Assist in Eliminating Obstacles

When tackling a new topic, try inputting a chapter of your study material into an AI chatbot and ask it to organize a multi-level outline for you. While the AI-generated outline may not be perfect, it can serve as a foundation for further organization. Interestingly, an imperfect AI outline provides a unique learning opportunity: after thoroughly reading the material, you can refine the outline, verifying your learning results in the process of identifying and correcting mistakes.

Beyond outlines, AI can help organize learning materials in various ways:
- Generate summaries, which you can modify to align with your understanding
- Extract key points from articles, potentially highlighting aspects you might have overlooked

When encountering unfamiliar terms or definitions, AI can save you considerable time searching for information. Simply send the challenging material to AI and request an explanation in simple, direct language. If you don't fully grasp its answer, ask for alternative explanations until you're satisfied with your level of understanding. While AI's responses may not always be 100% accurate, the immediate explanations it provides can serve as stepping stones for continued learning.

With AI's assistance, we can thoroughly study more materials. However, it's crucial to remember that no tool can replace our own efforts. This is due to how our brains function: information that enters without resistance is easily discarded. Without personal effort, we cannot transform external knowledge into our own. Using AI to assist learning is not about replacing our efforts, but about allowing us to invest our time and energy in real challenges.

AI can also help eliminate learning obstacles related to action. If you aim to master a skill, AI can transform theoretical knowledge from books into operational steps, enabling faster acquisition of practical skills. By informing AI about difficulties or errors encountered during execution, it can provide immediate suggestions and outline step-by-step procedures.

Using AI to Assist in Deepening Understanding

AI can be a valuable tool for enhancing our understanding of learning material. One effective method is to have AI generate questions based on your study content to assess your knowledge mastery. You can tailor questions to your specific needs, turning AI into an interactive teacher that evaluates your level and answers your questions during the assessment. Here's a prompt template you can use:

Prompt: Based on the following material, divide the knowledge into three levels: easy, medium, and difficult. Create five multiple-choice questions for each level. Send me the questions one by one, from easy to difficult. If I answer correctly twice, upgrade to a higher-level question. If I answer incorrectly, please provide the correct answer, explain it to me, and create another question on this knowledge point.

Keep in mind that AI-generated questions may sometimes contain errors or omissions, so remain vigilant. If you suspect an error, challenge it directly: "Is there an error in this question?" Engaging in this dialogue with AI can be a valuable learning experience.

Another way to deepen understanding is by explaining the content you're learning in your own words and sending it to AI for feedback. AI can comment on and fill in any gaps in your explanation. You can continue the dialogue by asking it to evaluate your revised answers and provide suggestions for improvement.

A more creative approach involves learning by teaching. Here's how it works: 1) You ask a question; 2) AI provides an answer; 3) You act as the teacher and evaluate whether AI's response is correct.

You can use this prompt as a template:

Prompt: You (AI) are a student who has already studied topic X, and the interlocutor plays the role of the teacher. Please follow these requirements:
- Think step-by-step and reflect on each step before making decisions.
- The purpose of this exercise is for the interlocutor to evaluate your explanations and applications.
- The interlocutor will send you concepts they want you to explain; you only need to wait until then.
- After receiving the concept requested by the interlocutor, you need to do the following:
  - Write three paragraphs explaining this concept and provide two application examples.
  - Ask the teacher how your answer is, what you did right or wrong, and how you can improve.
  - Ask how they think this concept should be better applied.

This exercise cleverly leverages AI's ability to generate text based on training materials, allowing you to improve your cognitive skills by correcting AI's "mistakes."

Using AI to Assist in Accelerating Output

Dedicated learners know that output is a highly effective learning method. By leveraging AI's language understanding and generation capabilities, we can significantly streamline the output process.

For instance, while reading a book, you might make numerous excerpts and notes. AI can help organize these excerpts by combining content, completing entries, or even rewriting them. It can also find related entries and link them together to form larger entries.

When writing notes or documents, consider that your future self will be the primary reader. Over time, memories may fade, making it difficult to understand past notes. Writing from another person's perspective with all necessary information ensures clarity later on. AI can facilitate this process by converting your content into a teaching style draft for further editing.

Overall, in terms of eliminating obstacles, deepening understanding, and accelerating output, AI is a powerful universal learning tool. By using AI wisely, achieving a tenfold improvement in learning effectiveness is possible.

After extensively using AI, you'll likely find that it greatly boosts your learning confidence. On one hand, it explains difficult points clearly, lowering barriers to new knowledge; on the other hand, it allows you to focus more time and energy on challenging areas, making them easier to tackle. This dual effect empowers learners to confidently say: "I can learn it!"—a sentiment shared by many who use AI as a learning aid.

Insight: Dancing with AI's Imperfections

You've likely noticed our consistent emphasis: AI's answers can be wrong. This is because generative AI doesn't simply perform direct database retrieval. Instead, it makes probabilistic predictions based on its vast "learned" data, responding in coherent sentences. To enable generation, we must loosen constraints and can't demand that every sentence it produces comes directly from original sources.

As AI's "learning" database expands and its capabilities rapidly evolve, the frequency of erroneous answers will decrease. However, we still need to verify AI's responses in practice before accepting them.

Key Points of This Chapter:
1. The 10X Principle: Each new type of technological tool can potentially improve learning efficiency at least tenfold when used effectively.
2. The main practical method of generative AI is: you ask, it answers. AI can serve as your teaching assistant, helper, and advisor.
3. AI can enhance learning effectiveness in three aspects: eliminating obstacles, deepening understanding, and accelerating output.
4. Be alert to errors in AI's answers and carefully verify the accuracy of AI responses yourself.

Practical Exercises:
1. Register and use several AI products.
2. Ask 10 questions at once and write down 3 impressions from your use of AI.
3. Use AI to complete a real task, such as:
    - Replying to an email
    - Revising an article you've written

- Translating a professional article

Part 2 Four Elements of Penetration Learning

Chapter 3: How to Obtain Your Own Knowledge System

Richard Feynman, the renowned Nobel Prize-winning physicist, left an intellectual legacy that extends far beyond the scientific community. Known as the "scientific prankster," Feynman developed several unique and effective learning methods that have been widely adopted by learners across various fields. Let's explore how we can cleverly apply Feynman's learning methods to study a topic and acquire its knowledge system.

Defining the "Domain Knowledge Boundary" for Topic Learning

One of the primary challenges in modern learning is the interconnectedness of information, leading to an exponential growth in the amount of knowledge compared to decades ago. Faced with this seemingly endless expanse of information, learners might feel overwhelmed before even beginning their journey. To combat this, our first task when undertaking topic learning is to define the "domain knowledge boundary" - essentially outlining the scope of our learning.

We have three options when defining this boundary:
1. Include all content we encounter within the domain knowledge boundary.
2. Select a relatively small range where the knowledge structure and points are clear and distinct.
3. Choose a moderately sized range that allows for exploration but requires some trade-offs compared to the first option.

The third option not only considers the scope's size but also demonstrates the learner's judgment. When first encountering a topic, we're presented with a dazzling array of knowledge points. As we expand our horizons and acquire information, certain hot topics naturally attract our attention. However, through further exploration, we may find that some of these trending subjects are not truly important, leading us to exclude them from our defined boundary.

When defining the domain knowledge boundary, we briefly organize the knowledge points we understand and integrate similar content blocks. After this integration, we often discover that some content blocks and key knowledge share similar forms.

Obtaining the Knowledge System

So, how do we obtain the knowledge system of this subject area? A simple and effective approach is to "copy" an existing knowledge system.

Hierarchical Outline: The Form of Knowledge System

With the help of tools like AI, we can search for knowledge systems about the topic we're learning. These systems come in various forms: mind maps, knowledge outlines, PPT presentations, etc. The simplest and most effective form is the tree structure we mentioned earlier.

A hierarchical outline representing the knowledge system typically includes:
1. Topic name and a one-sentence description (tree name)
2. Several subtopics and corresponding explanations (trunk, first-level items)

3. Main knowledge points of subtopics (main branches, second-level items)

You can further break down subtopics into finer knowledge points according to your needs.

Books provide an excellent example of knowledge organization through their table of contents, essentially a knowledge outline composed of "book title - chapters - sections". This is a knowledge system you can adapt for your own learning. Additionally, course outlines from online courses, paper reviews, and learning notes shared online are all valuable sources of outline information. It's recommended to compare several outlines before making a choice.

When organizing the knowledge system into your own hierarchical outline, avoid simply copying and pasting. Re-enter it word by word, making necessary adjustments according to your situation.

Ensure that your knowledge outline fits on a regular-sized printed paper or a horizontal screen. If it doesn't fit, you may have defined too large a scope or included overly detailed content. Printing out the outline and keeping it at hand can serve as a valuable learning tool, allowing you to grasp the outline as a whole and make convenient marks with a pen.

Feynman Blank Notebook: Your Empty Textbook

This method consists of three steps:
1. Write down the knowledge system of your chosen subject area in the form of a hierarchical outline on one page.
2. Expand the knowledge outline in a blank notebook. Imagine your notebook is an empty book, write the table of contents on the first page, and each subsequent page with a chapter or section title.
3. Use this notebook as a tool, learn each knowledge point, then explain it to others in your own words, gradually filling the blank notebook.

You can expand the outline in a thin blank notebook, create a document with blanks on your computer, or use software like Goodnotes on a tablet. For long-term topic studies, a tangible notebook that's always accessible can be an excellent learning tool, reducing mental load and minimizing distractions.

Feynman Technique: Learning by Teaching

The widely circulated "Feynman technique" promotes learning by teaching. It includes five steps:
1. Learn: Choose a knowledge point to study.
2. Explain: Explain this knowledge point to others in simple language.
3. Self-evaluate: Discover your own lack of understanding through teaching others.
4. Supplement: Go back to re-learn for better understanding.
5. Simplify: Simplify the learned knowledge point to deeply imprint it in your mind.

The second step is crucial, involving explaining the concept to someone unfamiliar with it using simple language. In the fourth step, you continue learning to address knowledge gaps. This cycle continues until you truly master the knowledge point.

The "Feynman Blank Notebook Method" and "Feynman Technique" serve different purposes:

the former is for overall learning, emphasizing the knowledge system, while the latter focuses on individual knowledge points, emphasizing learning by teaching.

When explaining concepts using simple language, avoid oversimplification. Instead, focus on:
1. Accuracy of expression
2. Avoiding professional jargon
3. Breaking down problems into basic steps or core frameworks
4. Explaining knowledge points through specific application examples

Practical Tips for Using the "Feynman Technique"

1. Develop your own Feynman technique explanation method:
   - Explain a concept in 90 seconds, as if to classmates
   - Clarify the learning question and provide a one-sentence answer before explaining
   - List an explanation outline with five key points

- Practice explaining with timing, aiming to improve within three attempts
2. Utilize technology to enhance explanations:
    - Record your explanation and review the video to identify unclear parts while improving presentation skills
    - Explain concepts to AI and request evaluations and suggestions
    - Ask AI to design explanations for specific target audiences and draft explanation outlines

Key Points of This Chapter:
1. Define the domain knowledge boundary for effective topic learning, as it determines subsequent learning arrangements and effectiveness.
2. Begin learning a topic by adapting an existing knowledge system.
3. Utilize Feynman's two learning methods: Feynman Blank Notebook and Feynman Technique.

Practical Exercises:
1. For a previously studied topic:

- Use a hierarchical outline to organize its knowledge system
- Write a knowledge outline based on your understanding
- Find an existing outline and compare the differences

2. For a new topic you want to learn:
   - Find an existing knowledge outline
   - Assess how much of this outline you can understand

3. Apply the Feynman technique:
   - Spend 30 minutes learning a knowledge point
   - Study the concept, then explain it to others
   - Identify knowledge gaps revealed during your explanation
   - Fill in these gaps through further study

Chapter 4: Deep Replication: How to First Quickly Understand 70%

The Entire Process of Thoroughly Learning a Subject Area

The journey to completely master a subject can be divided into five main stages:

1. **Initial Preparation Stage:** Clarify the starting point and define learning boundaries. Through preliminary learning, understand the overview, clarify main issues, and set learning goals.
2. **Knowledge System Stage:** Copy an existing knowledge outline and comprehensively study a textbook to master its content. This is where deep replication comes into play.
3. **Key In-depth Stage:** Conduct in-depth study of difficult points and doubts. (Chapters 5-9 will discuss specific methods such as rapid learning, efficient reading, and learning technical tools.)
4. **Output Understanding Stage:** Promote understanding through various forms of

output, including exams, papers, reports, and writing a personal knowledge guide. (Detailed in Chapter 10)
5. **Personal Innovation Stage:** For ambitious learners, compile learned knowledge into personal innovative works and products valuable to others.

Deep Replication in the Learning Stage

"Deep replication" refers to finding a "textbook" that can serve as a guide for the learning topic, aiming to understand 70% of it. Here, "textbook" broadly refers to all available learning materials.

This process involves five sub-steps:
1. **Intensive Reading:** Read every word and page carefully, trying to understand all unclear points.
2. **Redoing:** Retell, reason, and recreate formulas using your own understanding. Complete exercises and tests to objectively assess your level.
3. **Practice:** Recreate diagrams and charts; for technical learning, engage in hands-on practice.

4. **Recompiling the Textbook:** Based on your learning progress, create your own new textbook by adding materials and personal understanding.
5. **Reteaching:** Switch to the role of a teacher, using your new textbook as lecture notes to explain concepts to others.

Sponge Thinking, Slowing Down, and Mastering the Basics

The five-step deep replication method helps quickly understand 70% of the learning topic, laying the foundation for further learning. This stage requires a "sponge mindset" - absorbing all information comprehensively without selection.

Intensive reading, redoing, and practice emphasize slowing down the learning speed for better knowledge grasp. Converting content formats (e.g., inputting book content into notes, transforming text into outline-style lists) can also aid in viewing content from different perspectives.

Our goal is to understand 70%, temporarily labeling the remaining 30% as "don't know" for later study. This approach involves multiple rapid cycles through the learning process, a key feature of the penetration learning method.

When selecting a textbook, books from formal publishers are generally preferred for their higher quality. For digital materials, those with continuous iterations and large version numbers often indicate high quality.

Compiling Your Own Textbook and Teaching Yourself

In the five steps of deep replication, recompiling and reteaching are crucial for achieving optimal learning results.

When recompiling the textbook, follow the principle of "only add, don't subtract". At this stage, avoid judging what's important or ignorable. However, during the reteaching stage, you can break free from this constraint. As Bruce Lee said, "Absorb what is useful, discard what is useless, and add what is specifically your own." This is when you'll "discard what is useless" and "add what is specifically your own", truly internalizing the knowledge.

While this learning process may seem energy-intensive, the time and effort invested are worthwhile. The five steps of deep replication help lay a solid knowledge foundation for your chosen topic.

Learning by teaching others is an increasingly popular concept. In the "reteaching" step, explain the topic in detail using your newly compiled textbook or condensed lecture notes. After explaining each knowledge point, you'll likely notice a significant improvement in your understanding. Recording your explanation allows for self-evaluation and identification of areas needing improvement.

For those with additional time and energy, consider transcribing your reteaching content. While speaking is relatively easy, transforming speech into logically clear written text is more challenging but highly rewarding. This process makes your knowledge more precise and helps verify your learning level.

The penetration learning method compresses the learning cycle significantly. Under such time pressure, strategies and steps are crucial for completing learning tasks. Multiple rapid cycles align well with how our brains absorb and transform new knowledge.

Key Points of This Chapter:
1. Five steps of deep replication: intensive reading, redoing, practicing, recompiling, and reteaching.
2. Aim to understand 70% of the content in the knowledge outline.
3. Intensive reading: Read every word and page carefully.
4. Redoing: Redo explanations, reasoning, and formulas.
5. Practice: Recreate tables and diagrams, and perform practical operations.
6. Recompiling: Follow "only add, don't subtract" to create your new textbook.
7. Reteaching: Condense the new textbook into lecture notes and explain thoroughly.

Practical Exercise:
Choose a topic for a 6-hour study session using the five-step deep replication method:
- 1 hour each for intensive reading, redoing, practicing, and recompiling
- 1 hour for reteaching preparation

- 1 hour for actual explanation

Observe how your learning effectiveness changes throughout this process.

Chapter 5: Deep Sprint - How to Learn Thoroughly in Five Days

After intensively learning a topic using an existing knowledge outline and the five-step deep replication method, you face several potential paths:

1. Cease learning, satisfied with your current knowledge level. This choice may indicate the "Dunning-Kruger effect," where low-ability individuals overestimate their abilities.
2. Embark on extensive learning, recognizing more unknowns and related topics.
3. Adopt fragmented learning methods to "hunt" for knowledge, potentially leading to rich but shallow understanding.
4. Learn by doing, solidifying the knowledge system through teaching, creating questions, and applying skills to practical examples.

The last path is most suitable for smart learners. To facilitate this approach, we can use a sprint learning method adapted from the Design Sprint

used in product iteration. This method has two key characteristics:
- Maintains focus on mastering the overall knowledge system, arranging the learning process accordingly.
- Emphasizes "learning by doing," shifting from knowledge points to simulating future actions.

While the sprint learning method prioritizes speed, it adheres to basic learning logic, altering only specific practices. It's particularly effective for quickly learning unfamiliar fields, strategically breaking through learning obstacles.

Complete the Learning Loop in Five Days and Ten Steps

The sprint learning method comprises five days and ten steps:

1. **Day 1: Map Day**
   Set expectations or outcomes and obtain an overview map of the unfamiliar field.
2. **Day 2: Reconnaissance Day**
   Explore various possible learning paths.

3. **Day 3: Selection Day**
   Delve into difficult points and choose the optimal learning path.
4. **Day 4: Prototype Day**
   Practice and iterate the chosen path in a "sandbox" environment, creating a path prototype.
5. **Day 5: Submission Day**
   Present the path prototype to others and gather direct feedback.

This five-day sprint learning method is versatile, applicable to various learning scenarios:
- Learning new subject knowledge
- Acquiring new technical skills
- Developing general work skills
- Understanding a new industry

It's particularly suited for practice-related topics and quickly familiarizing oneself with unfamiliar fields.

Implementing the Five-Day Sprint Learning Method

Day 1: Map Day

Step 1: Set expected outcomes

- Clearly define your learning goals
- Identify specific questions you need to answer
- Determine the form of your final learning outcome (e.g., notes, plans, articles, samples)

Step 2: Draw your own map

- Create a visual representation of the knowledge system
- Base it on existing outlines but personalize it to your understanding
- Include main topics, subtopics, and their relationships

Before starting, reconfirm:

- Clear domain knowledge boundaries
- Availability of necessary learning materials (e.g., introductory books, online resources)
- Measurable learning goals
- Suitability of the sprint method for your topic

Day 2: Reconnaissance Day

Step 3: Field reconnaissance

- Engage in hands-on learning with your expected outcomes in mind

- For example, if learning a new programming tool:
    - Read official documentation
    - Write a simple example program following tutorials
    - Attempt to solve a real problem using the tool

Step 4: Identify possible action paths

- Based on your initial attempts, identify several ways to achieve your learning goal
- Focus on knowledge points directly related to your problem
- Temporarily set aside unrelated information

Day 3: Selection Day

Step 5: Study key points, difficult points, and doubtful points

- Dive deep into the most relevant techniques or concepts
- For example, if learning social media management:
    - Study content creation techniques
    - Analyze successful accounts in your niche
    - Experiment with different posting strategies

Step 6: Select the optimal path
- Based on your deep study and experiments, choose the most effective approach
- Consider factors like efficiency, resource requirements, and alignment with your goals
- Mark this chosen path on your "map" from Day 1

Day 4: Prototype Day

Step 7: Create the first prototype - Explain the topic to others
- Prepare a TED-style presentation:
  - Focus on one main idea
  - Limit to about 18 minutes
  - Use concepts familiar to a general audience
  - Make your idea worth sharing

Step 8: Create the second prototype - Develop an execution plan
- Create a detailed, step-by-step plan to apply your learned knowledge
- For social media management example:
  - Outline content creation process
  - Plan posting schedule
  - Detail engagement strategies

- List tools and resources needed
- Ensure the plan fits on one page for easy reference

Day 5: Submission Day

Step 9: Present the prototype and listen to feedback
- Present both your TED-style talk and execution plan
- Gather feedback from peers or mentors
- Pay attention to areas of confusion or skepticism in your audience

Step 10: Review and decide on next actions
- Compare actual outcomes with expected outcomes from Day 1
- Identify gaps in your learning
- Plan next steps to address these gaps
- Reflect on the learning process itself and note improvements for future sprints

Key Points of This Chapter:

1. The sprint learning method completes topic learning in five structured days and ten steps.

2. It focuses on scope, shortens the learning cycle, integrates learning and doing, and quickly completes a learning loop.
3. This method is particularly effective for rapidly familiarizing oneself with unfamiliar fields.
4. The process balances big-picture understanding with practical application.

Practical Exercise:
Choose a topic you want to learn and spend 30 minutes planning a sprint learning approach:
1. Define the overall expected outcome
2. Outline your approach for each of the five days and ten steps
3. Specify expected outcomes for each step

Write down your plan, including the overall expected outcome, approach for each step, and expected outcomes per step. Consider potential challenges and how you might overcome them.

Chapter 6: How to Improve Through Deliberate Practice

You've likely encountered the famous "10,000-hour rule" - the notion that repeating something for 10,000 hours can transform a novice into an expert. While this rule emphasizes the time and quantity of practice, we now understand that the quality of practice is the true key to improvement. Simply spending time on an activity is what psychologist Anders Ericsson calls "Naive Practice." What genuinely enhances our personal level is deliberate practice, which builds upon "purposeful practice."

Understanding the Evolution of Practice

- Naive Practice
  - Repeatedly doing something hoping repetition alone will improve performance
  - Often results in "treading water" rather than true improvement

- Purposeful Practice
  - Has specific goals
  - Emphasizes focus

- Includes feedback
- Requires practitioners to step out of their comfort zone

■ Deliberate Practice

Builds on purposeful practice with two key additions:
- Mentor guidance: Mentors understand expert-level performance, its underlying reasons, and the thought processes involved. These mentors can be individuals or excellent works in the field.
- Focus on Mental Representations: Using our brains to imagine every detail of an action, training through repeated visualization of the process.

Exercise 1: Practice Under Mentor Guidance

To implement deliberate practice, follow these steps:
1. Identify expert-level performers in your field
2. Study their performance and methods
3. Train under the guidance of mentors who understand expert performance

Example: Improving Social Media Growth
1. Find five top-performing accounts in your niche
2. Collect their 20 most successful videos from the past three months
3. Analyze each video for:
    - Caption style
    - Opening sentence structure
    - Transition techniques
    - Background music choices
    - Hashtag usage
    - Caption formatting
4. Apply your analysis:
    - Adapt their techniques to your content
    - Create and publish videos using these strategies
5. Evaluate results:
    - Compare your video performance with your "mentors'" data
    - Analyze improvements in views, interactions, and follower growth
    - Identify which techniques are most effective for your account
6. Iterate and refine your approach based on these insights

Practical Tip: Written Comparison Method
1. Write down your expected results
2. After six months, compare actual results with your written expectations
3. Analyze the gaps between expected and actual outcomes

This written method is crucial because:
- Human memory is often unreliable
- Seeing a tangible before-and-after comparison reveals true progress
- Understanding these differences enables meaningful adjustments and improvements

By following these deliberate practice techniques and consistently evaluating your progress, you can accelerate your learning and skill development far more effectively than through naive practice alone.

Exercise 2: Visualize Knowledge

To better master knowledge, tools, or skills, transforming existing information into visual charts is an effective practice method. Knowledge presented in an intuitive form is often easier to understand.

Ways to visualize knowledge include:
1. **Text to Lists or Tables:** Convert large paragraphs into lists, multi-level lists, or tables for a small step toward visualization.
2. **Hierarchical Mind Maps:** Transform lists into mind maps for a semi-visual representation.
3. **Simple Diagrams:** Use simple and clear diagrams to display content relationships based on logical connections.
4. **Complex Diagrams:** Create complex diagrams that reflect the intricate logic of the content.
5. **Infographics:** Organize content into large-scale diagrams such as infographics for comprehensive visualization.

Exercise 3: Create a Minimum Viable Product (MVP)

The concept of a Minimum Viable Product involves creating a simple prototype using minimal resources before investing heavily in the final product. This approach emphasizes creating something functional as early as possible.

This idea aligns with the penetration learning method's rapid cycles. First, quickly cover the learning topic as a whole, even if some aspects remain unclear. This process helps identify weak points for targeted learning.

Example: Writing

"Write fast, edit slow" is a method used by many successful writers. Often, writers struggle with inspiration or starting points. AI tools can help spark ideas, enabling you to quickly draft your work. This stage focuses on capturing ideas and establishing structure and logic, while local imperfections are secondary. The slow editing stage refines these details, turning the draft into your "something that can run."

Practical Tip: News Release MVP

In learning, assume tasks are completed and write a news release as if announcing them:
- Before writing an article, post an introduction on social media.

- Before writing a report or paper, draft an email introducing it to others.
- Before advancing a plan, describe its expected results to AI and request evaluation.

Exercise 4: Learn Publicly Online

To quickly get correct answers on social networks, consider posting an incorrect answer. People love correcting mistakes and will often provide the correct information in comments.

In the digital age, we can leverage practice methods that reflect digital characteristics by writing what we've learned and publishing it online. This approach connects you with online learning communities and provides feedback in a collaborative atmosphere. Publicly sharing your learning also motivates you to produce quality work. While your shared content might contain errors, corrections will soon follow.

To improve learning effectiveness, avoid mainstream social media to reduce pressure from traffic and likes and minimize distractions from constant information pushes. Instead, use note-

taking software to write and share complete note entries:
- Invite feedback from your learning group before making notes public
- Share unfinished notes rather than completed articles
- Seek advice rather than likes

This approach aligns with learning goals by encouraging constructive feedback rather than validation.

In the penetration learning method, various outputs can be shared as notes:
- Detailed outlines
- Book excerpts or class notes
- Organized key points and doubts
- Introductory tutorials, course PPTs, operation standards
- Personal knowledge guides

Practice Mindset: Use Vivid Metaphors

When applying knowledge to solve recurring problems, we often convert it into explicit form knowledge, creating tutorials, courses, or standards for ourselves and others to follow.

However, when facing new problems and unpredictable situations, we should transform our learning into a Mindset that guides us through the unknown.

Using vivid metaphors to demonstrate thinking modes can convert abstract thoughts into tangible concepts, making the invisible visible. This approach serves as an excellent thinking tool.

Benefits and Limitations of Metaphors

Vivid metaphors can significantly aid in exploring the unknown. However, it's crucial to:
1. Understand their strengths
2. Be aware of their limitations
3. Recognize that some metaphors may not be entirely accurate in all contexts

Practical Tip: Leveraging AI for Metaphor Creation

Utilize AI's capabilities to enhance your metaphorical thinking:
1. Ask AI to provide a series of related metaphors for your topic

2. Use AI's image generation abilities to visualize these metaphors

This approach can offer fresh perspectives and stimulate creative thinking.

Key Points of This Chapter:
1. Three types of practice:
    - Naive practice
    - Purposeful practice
    - Deliberate practice (emphasizing mentor guidance and mental representations)
2. Four methods of deep practice:
    - Practice under mentor guidance
    - Visualize knowledge
    - Create a Minimum Viable Product (MVP)
    - Learn publicly online
3. Use vivid metaphors to connect known scenarios with unknown fields, aiding exploration

Practical Exercises:
1. **Knowledge Visualization:**
   Choose a topic you're currently learning. Find a key diagram (logic diagram or flow

chart) related to this topic. Remake this diagram, incorporating your own understanding and insights.

2. **Metaphor Exploration:**
   a. When facing the unknown, what's the first metaphor that comes to your mind?
   b. To approach the unknown more confidently, brainstorm new metaphors that could replace your initial one. Consider how these new metaphors might change your perspective or approach.

3. **AI-Assisted Metaphor Generation:**
   Use an AI tool to generate multiple metaphors for a concept you're struggling to understand. Evaluate these metaphors and select the one that resonates most with you. Explain why this metaphor is particularly effective in enhancing your understanding.

4. **MVP Creation:**
   Choose a project or idea you've been considering. Create a Minimum Viable Product for it within a short timeframe (e.g., 24 hours). Reflect on what you learned from this rapid prototyping process.

5. **Public Learning Challenge:**
   Select a topic you're currently studying. Create a short post or article about it and

share it on a public platform (e.g., a blog, social media, or learning community). Engage with the feedback you receive and document how this public learning experience impacts your understanding and motivation.

Part 3: Three Scenarios for Penetration Learning

Chapter 7: Penetrative Reading: How to Read a Book Thoroughly

The importance of reading is self-evident. For those who enjoy a diverse range of books, the challenge is learning how to read thoroughly. The development of various AI tools has opened up new possibilities for enhancing our reading practices.

In this chapter, we will explore how to read using a sprint reading method that combines traditional techniques with modern tools. This method is suitable for in-depth reading of various materials, whether it be a book, several chapters, or other high-quality resources.

The sprint reading method can be divided into three stages: overview reading, deep reading, and reading output, encompassing ten interconnected steps. Before starting, ask yourself: What purpose do I want to achieve? What results do I want to complete?

Sprint Reading Method: 10 Detailed Steps

1. **Outcome Setting:** Clearly define and record the desired reading outcomes.
2. **Hierarchical Outline:** Quickly grasp the overall structure by creating a hierarchical outline.
3. **Intensive Reading:** Carefully read every word, marking key and doubtful points.
4. **Detailed List:** Record the main content in lists or multi-level lists.
5. **Key Notes:** Supplement learning through reading, searching, and questioning to deeply understand key points and write notes.
6. **Doubtful Point Notes:** Identify and resolve doubts or make corrections based on the reading content.
7. **Detailed Outline:** Create a comprehensive outline incorporating detailed lists, key notes, and doubtful point notes.
8. **Output Preparation:** Prepare for the outcome you set by selecting key points to explain to others.
9. **Display Output:** Present the completed outcome and evaluate it against your initial goals.

10. **Follow-up Tasks:** Address knowledge gaps, revise outcomes, and plan subsequent actions.

Consider the sprint reading method as a template suitable for high-quality materials across multiple disciplines and levels. Customize your approach based on the material you are reading, the tools you use, and your personal needs.

Techniques, Practices, and Tools in the Sprint Reading Method

The sprint reading method is designed for knowledge acquisition, problem-solving, mastering knowledge systems, and updating cognition. It requires in-depth engagement to understand nuances and connect knowledge with personal practice.

Selection of Reading Materials

Choose high-quality and systematic materials to minimize supplemental research during reading.

Pre-setting Outcomes

Set clear purposes and expected results before starting. For example, if your goal is "understanding methods in the book," your outcome might be "explaining methods in case form." Writing these down guides your reading process and helps verify goal achievement.

Speed Reading and Creating Hierarchical Outline

The first step in mastering a new subject is to gain a broad overview of the material. Begin by browsing through the book, paying particular attention to images, tables, chapter titles, bold words, and summaries. These elements often provide a quick snapshot of the key concepts and structure of the content.

As you browse, create an outline based on these elements using your preferred software tools. This initial outline serves as a framework for organizing the information you'll encounter during your more in-depth reading.

Next, engage in speed reading to grasp the overall content and logical structure of the material. As you speed read, update your outline with new information and insights. This process helps you build a comprehensive understanding of the subject matter while maintaining a bird's-eye view of its organization.

For physical books, consider using A4 paper or notebook pages for your outlines. Leave blank spaces between entries to accommodate keywords you'll identify during your speed reading session. This approach allows for flexibility and easy updates as you progress through the material.

Intensive Reading and Making Marks

After your initial overview, focus on the more challenging sections of the material by reading every word carefully. To enhance your understanding and retention, consider organizing the content into a PowerPoint presentation format. This visual approach can help clarify complex concepts and relationships.

When creating your PowerPoint-style notes:
- Organize content into discrete knowledge blocks, with one block per slide or page.

- Use color marks and diagrams to highlight important information and illustrate relationships between concepts.

This visual organization can significantly improve your ability to process and recall the information later.

Practical Tip: Let AI Help You "Translate" Complex Sentences

When encountering particularly difficult passages, leverage AI to simplify complex sentences. Use the following prompt:
"Please summarize the following meaning in one simple sentence for beginners."

This AI-assisted approach can help break down complex ideas into more digestible pieces, facilitating your understanding and retention of the material.

Organizing Detailed Content List

As you progress through your intensive reading, transform your excerpts into multi-level lists. Extract key sentences to create sub-items or abbreviate them into keywords. This process helps distill the information into a more manageable and easily reviewable format.

To gain a fresh perspective on your notes, consider using AI-supported speech synthesis to listen to them. This auditory review can help you identify potential issues or gaps in your understanding that might not be apparent when reading silently.

Studying Key Points and Writing Key Notes

To solidify your understanding of the material, focus on key content by:
- Redoing important derivations, whether they're argumentation processes or mathematical formulas.
- Using search engines and AI tools to find additional explanations or perspectives on complex topics.
- Considering practical applications of knowledge points through examples.

When helpful or necessary, draw diagrams to illustrate key content. Visual representations can often clarify relationships and processes that are difficult to grasp through text alone.

Write key notes that include problem descriptions, solutions, diagrams, and related materials. This process serves as a self-test of your mastery of the key content and creates a valuable resource for future review.

Practical Tip: Let AI Help You Write Draft Notes

To streamline your note-taking process, consider leveraging AI:

1. Send your material excerpts, scattered records, and note format requirements to an AI tool.
2. Request a draft note on relevant important knowledge points.
3. Review and refine the AI-generated draft by:
    - Correcting any errors
    - Improving the content
    - Optimizing expressions
4. Engage further with the AI by:
    - Asking for alternative explanations
    - Requesting different examples
    - Seeking revision suggestions

Remember, while AI can be a powerful tool in your learning process, always critically review and enhance the content it generates. AI-generated drafts may contain errors or misinterpretations, so your human insight and understanding remain crucial.

Solving Doubtful Points and Writing Doubtful Point Notes

Discovering and Solving Doubtful Points

As you study, you'll inevitably encounter areas of confusion or curiosity. Identify these doubtful points and resolve them by:
- Checking additional materials
- Consulting mentors or experts in the field
- Querying AI for clarification or additional information

Writing Doubtful Point Notes

While you'll likely encounter numerous minor doubts throughout your study, not all require extensive notes. Focus on doubts that relate to your unique learning experience or that significantly impact your understanding of the subject.

Consider writing notes when:
- The doubt relates to key content in the material
- The resolution provides valuable insights that enhance your overall understanding

These notes serve as a record of your learning process and can be invaluable when reviewing the material later.

Writing Detailed Outline

After collecting and processing information through the previous steps, it's time to integrate everything into a comprehensive outline. Begin with your initial outline and incorporate:
- Excerpt lists from your reading
- Key point notes
- Resolved doubtful points

Use office software or mind mapping tools to organize this content effectively. If organized properly, your detailed outline should resemble a lecture format, providing a clear and logical progression through the material.

For practical technical content, consider creating a step-by-step tutorial. This approach not only benefits others who might use your notes but also serves your future self when revisiting the material.

Preparing for Output

As you near the end of your study process, complete the expected output results in text form. The act of writing helps concretize ideas and often fosters creativity as you synthesize the information you've learned.

Create content that's easily accessible and iterable for future use. This might involve organizing your notes in a digital format, creating a personal wiki, or using a note-taking app that allows for easy searching and updating.

Displaying Output Results to Others

Set a personal deadline for displaying your reading output. Sharing your results with others serves multiple purposes:

- It improves learning efficiency by forcing you to articulate your understanding
- It enhances the completeness of your learning as others may point out areas you've overlooked
- It provides new perspectives by considering others' viewpoints on the material

By following this structured approach to learning, you'll not only gain a deep understanding of the subject matter but also develop valuable study skills that will serve you well in future learning endeavors.

Summary and Follow-up Tasks

After displaying your results:
1. Identify and address knowledge deficiencies.
2. Revise and iterate on unsatisfactory parts immediately.
3. Conduct targeted in-depth thinking based on personal insights and feedback from others.
4. Set reminders to reread the book and your notes after a period of time.
5. Create an action list to practice what you've learned from the book.

Additional Follow-up Suggestions:
- Schedule regular review sessions to reinforce key concepts.
- Identify practical applications of the knowledge in your daily life or work.
- Join or create a discussion group to explore the book's ideas further.
- Consider teaching the material to others to deepen your understanding.

Sprint Reading Method: 1-Hour Version

For shorter reading materials, you can simplify the sprint reading method into a 1-hour process. This condensed version is suitable for reading a book chapter or an independent report.

1-Hour Sprint Reading Process:

1. Set reading goals (2 minutes)
    - Example goal: Organize and explain the methods presented in the content
2. Overview the text (3 minutes)
    - Conduct a "text and image walk"
    - Write down section titles as first-level items in your outline

3. Intensive reading (20 minutes)
   - Read word-by-word at a relatively fast pace
   - Add main content to the outline as second and third-level items
   - Skip familiar content, case details, or additional information if time-constrained
4. Key content breakdown (10 minutes)
   - Choose one or two key concepts
   - Excerpt related content and organize into a list
5. Organize the outline (15 minutes)
   - Create a handout for explaining to others
   - Optional: Use AI to generate a speech draft based on your notes, then edit and revise
6. Practice explanation (10 minutes)
   - Explain for 5 minutes
   - Identify unclear parts
   - Adjust and re-explain for another 5 minutes

Key Points of This Chapter:

1. The sprint reading method applies the sprint learning approach to book reading, comprising ten steps:
   - Outcome setting
   - Hierarchical outline
   - Intensive reading
   - Detailed list
   - Key notes
   - Doubtful point notes
   - Detailed outline
   - Output preparation
   - Display output
   - Follow-up tasks
2. AI tools can assist in the reading process:
   - "Translating" complex sentences
   - Generating draft notes

Practical Exercises:
1. 1-Hour Sprint Reading Challenge:
   - Select a book chapter or short report
   - Apply the 1-hour sprint reading method
   - Record the time spent on each step
   - Document your insights and learning outcomes
2. Full Sprint Reading Method Application:
   - Choose a complete book

- Implement the full version of the sprint reading method
- After each step, record your thoughts and observations
- Reflect on how this method impacts your comprehension and retention

3. AI-Assisted Reading Experiment:
   - Select a challenging text
   - Use AI tools to assist with complex sentence interpretation and note drafting
   - Compare your understanding with and without AI assistance
   - Reflect on the benefits and limitations of AI in the reading process

4. Customized Sprint Reading Method:
   - Based on your experience with the provided method, create a personalized version that suits your reading style and goals
   - Test your custom method on various types of reading materials
   - Iterate and refine your approach based on results

5. Collaborative Sprint Reading:
   - Form a small group (2-3 people)

- Each member reads the same material using the sprint reading method
- Compare outlines, key points, and interpretations
- Discuss how different perspectives enhance overall understanding

Chapter 8: Penetrative Technology - How to Master a Technical Tool

In today's era, mastering technical tools is crucial. It not only enhances our efficiency but also ensures our cognitive skills keep pace with technological advancements.

However, many of us face a common problem: we start learning new skills or tools with enthusiasm, but after the initial excitement fades, we abandon most except for a few we use daily. What happens in between?

Challenges in Learning Technical Tools

Overwhelming Choices

The vast array of tools can be overwhelming. When starting a new skill or field, we often encounter numerous novel tools and see others using them effectively, prompting us to follow suit. We forget that these tools are merely means to an end, and not every tool will enhance our efficiency or help achieve our goals. This can lead to unnecessary workload, burnout, and eventual abandonment of the field.

Choosing Unsuitable Tools

The most valuable tools are those we can use daily, not necessarily the newest or most advanced. For novices, cutting-edge tools often require significant time and energy to learn, with many features being irrelevant at this stage. This can waste mental energy and lead to frustration.
Strategy for Mastering Technical Tools

Before mastering a tool, narrow your focus:
1. **Select Novice-Friendly Tools:** Choose tools that are easy to learn and relevant to your tasks.
2. **Master Relevant Features First:** Focus on mastering the parts of the tool most pertinent to your tasks before exploring peripheral features or considering upgrades.

The journey from beginner to proficient user is relatively short and obstacle-free. The real challenge lies in progressing from proficiency to mastery. Attempting to master all aspects of a tool at the outset is unrealistic. Instead, focus on completing specific tasks with the tool. As familiarity grows through actual use, mastery becomes more attainable.

How to Learn Technical Tools Step by Step

Determine the Scope of Application

Clarify two key questions before learning any technical tool:
1. What is the tool?
2. What is the task?

Read Documentation and Use Directly

When learning complex tools:
1. **Read Documentation:** Start with product manuals or beginner tutorials by expert users. For widely accepted tools, consider related books as alternatives.
2. **Use AI Assistance:** Employ AI to simplify documentation into direct usage steps.
3. **Practice Usage:** Follow examples in the documentation. If stuck, describe your

situation to an AI tool for advice based on previously read documents.

Follow Tutorials

Documentation alone may not suffice as tools often work with other components and require specific settings. Use online tutorials and examples as guides, akin to having an experienced mentor.

Try Single Point Breakthrough

After some experience, you may hit a plateau—beyond novice but not yet professional. Instead of relying solely on broad books like "From Entry to Mastery," consider these methods:
1. **Investigate Specific Questions:** For mastered features and tasks, delve deeper:
    - What's the principle behind this practice?
    - How can it be improved?
    - Are there simpler ways?
2. **Expand Single Points:** Master related features around what you know (e.g., if you know feature A, explore B, C, D) and combine them for application.

At this stage, you're closer to mastery than proficiency. Whether you achieve full mastery depends on your personal goals, determination, investment, and learning skills.

10 Concepts for Using Tools Well

1. **Focus on content, not tools:** Tools and skills are means; completing tasks is the purpose.
2. **Use task-relevant advanced tools:** Prioritize tools most relevant to the task over all-in-one solutions.
3. **Selective function usage:** When using powerful tools, focus on the most necessary functions rather than attempting to use all features.
4. **Master basic tools:** Learn tools essential for daily tasks (e.g., driving a car for commuting, not flying a helicopter).
5. **Use tools that suit you:** Find and personalize tools that fit your needs and use them consistently.
6. **Compromise in collaboration:** Adapt to tools used by work partners unless you can convince everyone to change collectively.

7. **Adopt new versions cautiously:** Use updated tools but avoid implementing brand new tools too early to prevent unnecessary complications.
8. **Maintain and update your toolbox:** Assemble a collection of tools and regularly update it, considering compatibility with existing tools.
9. **Deepen tool usage:** Strive to fully master at least one function each time you use existing or new tools.
10. **Seek efficiency multipliers:** Continuously look for tools that can significantly enhance your productivity, including AI tools.

Methods to Become a Tool Expert

To elevate your expertise, consider these three approaches:
1. Organize your knowledge into a beginner's tutorial
2. Design a training course based on your learning
3. Formulate operation standards from your experience

I. Organize What You've Learned into a Beginner's Tutorial

Writing a tutorial for others deepens your understanding by forcing you to consider operational details carefully. A beginner's tutorial typically includes:
- Simple, direct steps (e.g., Step 1: Action and result; Step 2; Step 3...)
- Detailed instructions for complex tasks

The process of creating a quality tutorial often requires multiple repetitions, enhancing your skills and uncovering previously overlooked details.

Updating Existing Tutorials

For rapidly evolving tools, consider updating existing online tutorials:
- Record step-by-step instructions for the latest version
- Create an updated tutorial based on current functionality

Understanding Tutorial Limitations

Beginner tutorials often simplify content compared to real-world applications. They provide a clear, linear path while ignoring complexities. As learners or tutorial creators, it's important to recognize this limitation and move beyond it.

Practical Tip: How to Write a Beginner's Tutorial

1. Introduction and Principles
- Choose a specific "how-to" topic
- Aim for concise, executable steps
- Ensure clear expected results for each step
- Consider iterating on existing tutorials
- Utilize AI assistance if desired

2. Six Steps to Write a Beginner's Tutorial

a. Topic Selection and Outline:
- Select a topic
- Outline key points
- Show expected results
- List prerequisites

b. Practical Operation:
- Perform the task
- Record detailed, ordered steps

c. Initial Review:
- Follow your steps from the beginning
- Adjust and optimize as needed

d. Streamline and Clarify:
- Simplify steps where possible
- Explain error-prone sections thoroughly

e. User-Centric Revision:
- Modify descriptions for user understanding
- Ensure operability and clear expected results

f. Final Polish:
- Proofread and adjust formatting
- Publish the first version
- Write summary and suggestions

By following these steps, you can create effective beginner tutorials while deepening your own understanding of the tool or process.

II. Design What You've Learned into a Training Course

Teaching others deepens our understanding of knowledge systematically. Compared to beginner's tutorials, training courses require:
- Deeper understanding of usage principles
- Overall perspective of the tool

- Knowledge of potential problems and solutions

Key aspects of course design:
1. **Goal-Oriented Structure:** Design the course outline based on tasks learners can complete after finishing.
2. **Practical Demonstrations:** Show results or comparisons rather than just explaining principles.
3. **Enhanced Engagement:** This approach makes courses more attractive and increases learners' sense of achievement.

III. Formulate What You've Learned into Operation Standards (SOP)

Standard Operating Procedures (SOPs) are norms for frequently executed actions, ensuring high-standard results.

Benefits of SOPs:
- Transform actions into habits
- Save time and mental energy
- Achieve consistently high-quality results
- Provide a basis for continuous improvement

Characteristics of good SOPs:

- Written from the user's perspective
- Detailed step-by-step instructions
- Include ideal results for comparison
- Continuously iterated to adapt to new situations

For more on this topic, refer to Atul Gawande's "The Checklist Manifesto."

Practical Tip: Self-Check Checklist for Effective Instructions

1. Explain through actual scenarios for better understanding
2. Describe both the process and significance of actions
3. Clearly mark error-prone areas
4. Include commonly overlooked "common sense" information
5. Provide necessary illustrations
6. Use simple, clear language; avoid complex jargon
7. Ensure content aligns with readers' cognitive habits

Key Points of This Chapter

1. Quick Tool Learning Strategy: Choose a practical operation and aim for mastery in that specific function.

2. Four Steps to Learning Tools:
   - Determine the scope of application
   - Read documentation and use directly
   - Follow tutorials
   - Attempt single point breakthrough
3. Concepts for Effective Tool Use:
   - Focus on tasks, not tools
   - Use tools most relevant to tasks
   - Master basic tools
   - Choose tools that suit you best
4. Three Steps to Becoming a Tool Expert:
   - Organize learning into a beginner's tutorial
   - Design a training course
   - Formulate operation standards

Practical Exercises

1. Tool Learning Reflection:
   - List 5 technical tools you've learned, in reverse chronological order
   - Review your work and study experience
   - Note 3 positive experiences and 3 common usage errors
2. Rapid Mastery Challenge:

- Choose a specific function of a software
- Learn to use it effectively within one day
- Aim for near-mastery level usage
- Record your learning process
- Reflect: If you could start over, how would you improve your approach?

3. SOP Creation:
   - Select a repetitive task in your work or study
   - Create a detailed SOP for this task
   - Test the SOP by having a colleague follow it
   - Refine based on feedback

4. Mini Training Course Design:
   - Choose a tool you're proficient with
   - Design a 30-minute training session
   - Include clear learning objectives, demonstrations, and hands-on practice
   - Deliver the session to a small group and gather feedback

5. Tool Ecosystem Analysis:
   - Map out the tools you use regularly
   - Identify any redundancies or gaps

- Research potential new tools to fill gaps or replace less efficient ones
- Create a plan to optimize your tool ecosystem

Chapter 9: Penetrative Questioning - How to Master Questioning Skills in the AI Era

The advent of generative AI has heightened the importance of questioning skills. As we can now ask AI questions at any time, the quality of our questions directly impacts the quality of the answers we receive. Moreover, as questioners, we must be able to critically evaluate the correctness and quality of AI's responses.

Relearning How to Ask Questions

While everyone can ask questions, not everyone has mastered the art of asking good questions. The essence of questioning skills lies in logical thinking ability. Let's explore this perspective as we relearn how to ask questions effectively.

Defining the Learning Boundary: Focusing on Evaluating Answers

The questions we discuss in this chapter fall into two main categories:

1. Questions about the unknown
2. Questions seeking something from the answerer

There are four main steps in asking question in this regard:
1. Identifying the real problem
2. Expressing the question clearly
3. Receiving the answer
4. Evaluating the accuracy and quality of the answer

Copying the Framework: Critical Thinker's Framework for Evaluating Answers

The authors of "Asking the Right Questions" propose that "as a critical thinker, your goal is to constantly pursue better conclusions, beliefs, and decisions."

They provide a framework for evaluating answers as critical thinkers:
1. What are the issue and conclusion?
2. What are the reasons?
3. Are there any ambiguous words?
4. What are the value assumptions and descriptive assumptions?

5. Are there any fallacies in the argumentation?
6. How strong is the evidence?
7. Are there alternative causes?
8. Is the data deceptive?
9. Is any important information omitted?
10. What other reasonable conclusions can be drawn?
11. What are the obstacles to critical thinking?

This framework helps us analyze information, recognize truth, form beliefs, and make better decisions. It can be used both to evaluate the quality of received answers and to provide more reasonable and powerful answers when questioned.

Key Exploration: Finding Assumptions and Adopting Gray Thinking

Understanding Assumptions

Assumptions, as defined in "Asking the Right Questions," come in two types:
1. Value assumptions (about what the world should be like)

2. Descriptive assumptions (about what the world was, is, or will be like)

Characteristics of assumptions:
- Hidden or unstated
- Taken for granted by the arguer
- Significantly impact the conclusion
- Potentially deceptive
- Necessary for reasons pointing to a specific conclusion

Finding Assumptions

A practical method for finding assumptions is to re-argue with existing materials. In the AI era, we can leverage AI's language and reasoning abilities for this process. Try asking AI: "What are the unstated assumptions in this discussion? Please list them one by one."

Adopting Gray Thinking

In our current era of easy information exchange, many extreme views represent black-and-white dichotomous thinking. Gray thinking—recognizing the nuanced area between extremes—is often necessary for finding optimal answers.

Practical Tips for Better Questioning

1. When using search engines, ask yourself: "If I continue searching, can I find new information leading to a better conclusion?"
2. When questioning AI, consider: "If I rephrase my question or add more specific instructions, can I get better answers?"
3. Always assume there are better answers—this mindset is key to obtaining high-quality information online.

By mastering these questioning skills and adopting a critical thinking approach, we can navigate the AI era more effectively, extracting valuable insights and making informed decisions.

The Value of Questions in the Age of AI

In our rapidly evolving technological landscape, the ability to ask meaningful questions has become more crucial than ever. As artificial intelligence continues to advance, finding answers to our queries becomes increasingly effortless, provided we know how to utilize the available resources effectively. However, the real challenge

—and indeed, the true value—lies in our capacity to identify and articulate meaningful problems to solve.

The Power of Problem Formulation

Kevin Kelly, a renowned technology writer, offers a valuable insight into problem-solving: "When you're stuck, explain your problem to someone else. Often, just by clearly stating the problem, the solution will surface. Make explaining the problem part of the process of solving difficult problems." This perspective aligns with Albert Einstein's famous assertion that "the formulation of the problem is often more essential than its solution."

These observations underscore a critical point: the process of identifying and articulating a problem is not merely a precursor to problem-solving—it is an integral part of the solution itself. By clearly defining the issue at hand, we often illuminate pathways to resolution that were previously obscured.

Critical Thinking and Problem Identification

Developing strong critical thinking skills is key to becoming adept at problem identification. When confronted with ambiguous arguments or complex situations, a systematic approach can be invaluable:

1. Employ a structured thinking framework to eliminate doubts and clarify the issue.
2. Leverage AI assistance to efficiently eliminate possibilities and narrow down the scope of the problem.
3. Systematically work through the remaining options to pinpoint the real problem at the core of the issue.

This methodical approach, combining human insight with AI capabilities, can significantly enhance our problem-solving efficacy.

Balancing Big Picture and Details: A Goal-Setting Strategy

Effective problem-solving and learning often require a balance between overall vision and granular focus. One way to achieve this balance is through a comprehensive goal-setting strategy

that combines big-picture thinking with attention to detail:
1. Set measurable goals across different time frames: current, short-term, medium-term, and long-term.
2. For each goal, assign a specific time range for completion.
3. List the necessary steps required to achieve each goal.
4. Transform these steps into specific, feasible actions.
5. Work towards your goals through continuous action at various stages.

This approach ensures that you maintain sight of your overarching objectives while making tangible progress through smaller, manageable tasks.

Applying the Penetration Learning Method

When tackling specific learning content, the penetration learning method offers a structured approach:
1. Conduct multiple rapid learning cycles to build familiarity with the material.
2. Organize a knowledge outline to gain an overall concept of the subject.

3. Identify difficult points and areas of doubt within specific knowledge areas.
4. Systematically address and overcome these challenges one by one.

This method allows for a comprehensive understanding of the subject matter, combining broad overview with focused problem-solving.

Leveraging AI for Efficient Task Completion

The vast knowledge database of AI presents a significant advantage in our learning and problem-solving endeavors. By mastering AI tools early and effectively, we can:

1. Surpass the knowledge and skills of those resistant to lifelong learning.
2. Achieve a "curve overtaking" in personal development, accelerating our growth and capabilities.

In conclusion, while AI has made answers more accessible than ever, the true value lies in our ability to ask insightful questions and identify meaningful problems. By honing our critical thinking skills, balancing big-picture goals with detailed actions, and leveraging AI tools effectively, we can navigate the complexities of our rapidly changing world with confidence and creativity.

8 Principles for Effective AI Questioning

To harness the full potential of AI tools, it's crucial to understand how to formulate questions effectively. The following principles will guide you in crafting queries that elicit accurate and useful responses, even if you're new to AI technology.

Principle 1: Understanding AI's Pattern Prediction

AI systems, like ChatGPT, don't think like humans. Instead, they predict patterns based on vast amounts of data they've been trained on. As Pam Baker explains in "ChatGPT Super Introduction": "ChatGPT doesn't think like humans, it predicts based on learned patterns, then organizes into sentences to answer based on predicted preferences and word order."

This pattern prediction underlies AI's abilities in:
- Language expression

- Code writing
- Knowledge retrieval
- Reasoning

Understanding this principle helps you:
1. Avoid blindly trusting AI responses, even if they sound fluent and well-formatted.
2. Recognize that AI capabilities are rapidly evolving, so don't underestimate their potential.

Principle 2: Being Alert to "Hallucinations" and Fact-Checking

AI can sometimes produce "hallucinations" - confidently stated but incorrect information. This is an inherent risk of AI's generative capabilities.

To mitigate this:
1. Always fact-check important information provided by AI.
2. Use critical thinking when evaluating AI responses:
    - Identify the main points and conclusions
    - Examine the reasoning and evidence provided

- Look for vague statements or hidden assumptions
- Check for logical errors
3. Use search engines or reliable sources to verify AI-generated information.

Principle 3: Using Structured Prompts

Structuring your questions or prompts can significantly improve AI responses. Include these components in your prompts:
1. Instruction:
    - Specify the role you want the AI to assume (e.g., "Act as a history teacher")
    - Clearly state the task or question
    - Provide any rules or constraints
2. Context:
    - Give relevant background information
    - Outline any steps or processes involved
    - Provide examples if helpful
3. Output Indicator:
    - Specify how you want the answer formatted
    - Indicate any performance criteria

For example, instead of asking "Tell me about climate change," you might say:

"Act as an environmental scientist. Explain the basics of climate change in simple terms. Include three main causes and three potential consequences. Format your response as a bulleted list."

Principle 4: Leveraging Few-Shot Prompting

When asking about topics the AI might not have extensive information on (like very recent events or specialized content), use few-shot prompting:

1. Provide context and examples in your prompt
2. Specify the format you want for the output

For instance, if you're asking the AI to generate social media posts in a specific style:

"Here are three examples of Instagram captions for a coffee shop:

1. 'Monday motivation in a cup ☕ #CaffeineKick'
2. 'Latte art or masterpiece? You decide! 🎨'

3. 'Rainy days call for extra whipped cream 🌂'

Using these as inspiration, create 3 new Instagram captions for a coffee shop, maintaining a similar style and tone."

By following these principles, even those new to AI tools can effectively harness their capabilities. Remember, practice and experimentation will help you refine your questioning techniques over time.

Principle 5: Encouraging "Chain of Thought" and Slow Thinking Mode

Mathematical reasoning and complex problem-solving can be challenging for AI models. To improve accuracy and reliability in these areas, consider the following strategies:
1. Use "Chain of Thought" prompts:
    - Add phrases like "Let's think step by step" or "Let's approach this systematically" to your prompt.
    - This encourages the AI to break down the problem and solve it incrementally.
2. Encourage inner monologue:

- Ask the AI to write down its analysis and reasoning process.
- For example, "As you solve this problem, please explain your thought process at each step."

This approach often leads to significantly improved answer correctness, as it mimics human problem-solving techniques and allows you to follow the AI's reasoning.

Principle 6: Breaking Down Complex Tasks into Simpler Subtasks

When faced with complex tasks, consider these two effective strategies:
1. Self-breakdown method:
    - Divide the task into specific points or subtasks yourself.
    - Ask the AI questions about each point separately.
    Benefits:
    - You'll receive more precise answers.
    - It's easier to fact-check individual components.
2. Guided breakdown method:

- Include task completion steps in the prompt's context.
- Direct the AI to follow these steps.
- Iterate and refine the steps for continuous improvement.

For example, instead of asking "How do I start a business?", break it down:
"Let's discuss starting a business step by step:
1. What's involved in market research?
2. How do I create a business plan?
3. What are the legal requirements for registering a business?
   Please address each point separately."

Principle 7: Inputting Information in Model-Friendly Formats

To optimize data input for better AI comprehension and more accurate responses:
1. Use special separators for long texts:
   - Enclose paragraphs with triple quotation marks ("""paragraph""")
2. Emphasize key information:
   - Use quotation marks ("") for important words or phrases.

- Add brackets (this is important) after crucial elements.
3. Adopt structured markings:
    - Number main points (part 1, part 2, part 3)
    - Use sub-numbering for details (1.1, 1.2, 1.3)
    - Separate multiple samples with line breaks instead of periods.
4. Borrow from programming principles:
    - Strive for clarity and conciseness in your prompts.
    - Follow the "Don't Repeat Yourself" (DRY) principle to avoid redundancy.

For example:
"""Please analyze this marketing strategy:
Part 1: Target audience
1.1 Demographics
1.2 Psychographics
Part 2: Channels
2.1 Social media (this is important)
2.2 Email marketing
Part 3: "Key messaging""""

Principle 8: Maintaining Control and Collaborating with AI

As AI tools rapidly evolve, it's crucial to maintain perspective and use them effectively:
1. Address common concerns:
   - Understand that while AI may change job landscapes, it also creates new opportunities.
   - Recognize that AI is a tool designed to assist, not replace or harm humans.
   - Be aware of privacy considerations when using AI tools.
2. Adopt a proactive mindset:
   - Focus on learning advanced AI usage skills to stay ahead.
   - Exploit AI's maximum potential for efficient task completion.
3. Redefine your role:
   - View yourself as the main character in your work or projects.
   - Consider AI as your co-pilot, strategist, personal assistant, and tutor.
4. Embrace a developmental perspective:

- Concentrate on creative, challenging, and fulfilling tasks that showcase human ingenuity.
- Let AI handle repetitive or data-intensive tasks where it excels.

5. Take responsibility for your future:
    - Recognize that your choices and actions shape your path, not AI.
    - Use AI as a tool to enhance, not replace, your capabilities.

By following these principles, you can effectively harness AI's power while maintaining control and focusing on tasks that truly require human creativity and insight.

Key Points of This Chapter

1. The Value of Questions:
    - Questions are often more valuable than answers
    - Critical thinking helps in problem discovery
2. Critical Thinking Framework:

    Analyze answers or opinions using the 11 elements from "Asking the Right Questions":
    - Issue

- Conclusion
- Reasons
- Word Meaning
- Assumptions
- Argumentation
- Evidence
- Alternative Causes
- Data
- Omitted Information
- Other Possible Conclusions
3. Stages of Questioning:
    - Discovering problems
    - Defining problems
    - Solving process
    - Answering
4. Skill Development:
    - Continuously hone problem discovery abilities
    - Use AI to assist in employing the elimination method for identifying real problems

Practical Exercises
Exercise 1: Critical Analysis of Non-Fiction
1. Select a non-fiction book
2. Choose an argument from the book

3. Analyze the argument using the 11 elements of critical thinking
4. Reframe your perspective:
   - Re-explain the argument using your own thoughts
   - Check your explanation against the 11 elements
   - Refine until your explanation is robust

Exercise 2: Problem Identification in Your Learning Topic
1. List 10 questions related to your current learning topic
2. Apply the elimination method:
   - Analyze each question systematically
   - Identify which question represents the real, core problem
   - Explain your reasoning for selecting this question

Exercise 3: AI-Assisted Problem Discovery
1. Choose a complex issue in your field of study or work
2. Use an AI tool to generate potential problems related to this issue
3. Apply the critical thinking framework to evaluate the AI-generated problems

4. Identify the most significant problem among them
5. Reflect on how AI assisted in broadening your perspective on the issue

Chapter 10: Writing a Personal Knowledge Guide to Enhance Cognition

As we approach the conclusion of our learning journey, a crucial question emerges: How do we effectively solidify our newly acquired knowledge and ensure that our cognitive abilities have significantly improved? The answer lies in creating a Personal Knowledge Guide, a comprehensive document that encapsulates the essence of your topic study.

This guide is not merely a collection of notes; rather, it's an evolved, structured representation of the knowledge system you've developed throughout your learning process. By summarizing and organizing what you've learned in the form of outlines and lists, you create a tangible record of your intellectual growth.

The Role of Personal Knowledge Guide

The Personal Knowledge Guide serves multiple purposes, each contributing to the deepening of your understanding and the enhancement of your cognitive abilities.

Firstly, it functions similarly to a literature review, providing a comprehensive overview of the subject matter. As you sort through the knowledge you've accumulated, you'll find yourself engaging with the material on a deeper level. This process of organization and synthesis helps to solidify your understanding and reveals connections between different aspects of the topic that may not have been apparent during the initial learning phase.

The guide's structure, typically in the form of outlines and lists, is deliberately chosen to facilitate quick completion and accelerate the learning cycle. This format aligns well with our learning objectives, allowing for easy reference and review. Unlike the scattered notes you might have taken during the learning process, the Personal Knowledge Guide presents a cohesive, structured view of the entire knowledge system you've built.

It's important to note that you are the primary audience for this guide. As you delve deeper into your topic of study, you'll accumulate a vast amount of knowledge, information, and personal insights. The process of writing the guide involves organizing and summarizing all of this information into a more structured hierarchical outline. This outline should highlight key points, strike a balance between detail and conciseness, and be comprehensible to others if needed.

During the writing process, you'll likely find yourself establishing more connections between different knowledge points. New ideas may emerge as you see the information laid out in a structured format. This cognitive synthesis is one of the most valuable aspects of creating a Personal Knowledge Guide, often leading to a significant deepening of your understanding. In fact, this phase of the learning process typically offers the highest input-output ratio, making it an invaluable part of your study.

Suggestions for Writing Personal Knowledge Guide

When approaching the task of writing your Personal Knowledge Guide, it's crucial to understand that this is not just a summary of what you've learned, but a tool for further learning and cognitive enhancement. The guide represents your organization of the knowledge acquired about a specific learning topic, serving as a summary written to yourself: "On this issue, this is what I've learned."

The optimal time to write your guide is immediately upon completing your learning content. At this juncture, your understanding of the material is at its peak, the information is still fresh in your mind, and you can maintain an objective, straightforward record of your knowledge.

Writing in List Form

The recommended structure for your Personal Knowledge Guide is a hierarchical outline, essentially writing in list form. This structure typically comprises three levels:
1. The first level consists of subtopics, providing a broad overview of the main areas within your subject.
2. The second level delves into the knowledge points of these subtopics, offering more specific information.

3. The third level provides detailed discussions of these knowledge points, exploring nuances and complexities.

It's crucial to ensure that these three levels of entries fully reflect the knowledge system of your subject area. To achieve this, consider using topic sentences and descriptive sentences to form each entry list. You can elaborate on the knowledge points under each subtopic using time-ordered steps or by enumerating key points.

This approach not only clarifies the logic of your knowledge structure but also aids in quickly sorting and integrating knowledge points into cohesive blocks. These knowledge blocks will help deepen your understanding of the topic and facilitate easier review and application of the knowledge you've acquired.

Avoiding Common Pitfalls

As you write your guide, be mindful of two common problems:

1. Excessive quotations: Remember, the primary nature of the Personal Knowledge Guide is that of private notes. Strive to use

your own words to articulate your understanding rather than directly excerpting content from learning materials. This process of rephrasing and explaining concepts in your own terms significantly enhances your grasp of the subject matter.
2. Repeatedly "reinventing the wheel": While your guide should primarily reflect your understanding, it doesn't need to be entirely original. If certain practices or concepts are widely accepted in your field of study, it's perfectly acceptable to include them in your guide for future reference. The key is to strike a balance between original insights and established knowledge.

By avoiding these pitfalls, you ensure that your Personal Knowledge Guide truly reflects your understanding and serves as an effective tool for future learning and application.

As we move forward, we'll explore practical methods for drafting your guide and strategies for continuous improvement, ensuring that your Personal Knowledge Guide becomes a living document that grows and evolves with your understanding.

Six Steps to Write a Personal Knowledge Guide:

1. *Select the topic*
   - Review the learned field, redefine the boundaries
   - Select the topic words and write down the title: "The Complete Guide to xxx"
   - Define a topic question
   - Write a one-sentence answer
   - Select writing tools and deadline
   - Set a target reader, which can be your friends or family around you, or your future self
2. *Write first-level entries*
   - List the key points that can be included in first-level entries
   - Write topic sentences and explanations for each entry
   - Think about the relationships between entries for overall grasp and memory
3. *Write second-level and third-level entries*
   - Write second-level entries for each first-level entry

- Write third-level entries in the form of ordered lists
- Supplement explanations after some entry topic sentences as needed
- When revising, enhance the expression accuracy of entries at all levels, and adjust the order and relationship of first-level and second-level entries as needed

4. *Switch to the target reader's perspective for editing*
   - Based on the previous step, readjust the order relationship and expression of first-level and second-level entries to make it easier for the audience to understand
   - Add necessary new entries from the audience's perspective

5. *Check and proofread entries*
   - Extract some first-level or second-level entries and try to explain to others using the Feynman technique
   - Check if any important knowledge points have been omitted
   - Check what knowledge points have changed but not updated here
   - Check for errors

- Highlight key points, cut redundancies
6. *Finalize and iterate*
    - Streamline the number of entries and the number of words for each entry
    - Convert formats (such as printing out) to check for logical errors and text omissions
    - Determine the version
    - Remember to come back for continuous iteration in the future

Practical Tips
- Use the document as a script to give a presentation
- Send the document to AI at different levels (questions and conclusions, outline, separate paragraphs, etc.) for opinions and suggestions

Key Points of This Chapter
1. The Personal Knowledge Guide as a Learning Summary:
    - Serves as the culmination of a topic study

- Progresses from initial outline to detailed outline, and finally to a comprehensive knowledge system record
2. Writing Suggestions for Personal Knowledge Guide:
    - Write in list form for clarity and easy reference
    - Avoid unnecessary repetition of established concepts
    - Engage in continuous iteration while maintaining a questioning attitude
3. Methods for Drafting:
    - Direct writing: Spontaneous capture of ideas and knowledge
    - Question-answering: Structured approach based on self-interrogation
    - Teaching approach: Explaining concepts as if instructing others
4. Six-Step Writing Process:
    - Select the topic and define its scope
    - Develop first-level entries (main concepts)
    - Expand with second-level entries (supporting details)
    - Edit from the target reader's perspective

- Thoroughly check and proofread content
- Finalize the guide and plan for future iterations

Practical Exercises

Exercise 1: Penetration Learning Method Guide

Create a personal knowledge guide on the "penetration learning method" discussed in this book:

1. List 7 concepts or methods from the book that you found particularly inspiring
2. Identify 7 learning concepts and methods that you personally find effective
3. Organize these insights into a structured guide using the list format

Exercise 2: Recent Learning Topic Guide

Choose a topic you've recently studied and create a complete guide following the "six steps of writing a personal knowledge guide":

1. Topic Selection:
    - Define the topic and its boundaries
    - Formulate a central question and a concise answer
2. First-Level Entries:
    - Identify key concepts or main sections

- Write topic sentences for each entry
3. Second-Level Entries:
   - Expand on first-level entries with supporting details
   - Organize information in a logical sequence
4. Reader-Centric Editing:
   - Revise content from your target reader's perspective
   - Ensure clarity and accessibility of information
5. Content Review:
   - Check for completeness and accuracy of information
   - Apply the Feynman Technique to test your understanding
6. Finalization:
   - Streamline content for conciseness
   - Plan for future updates and iterations

Exercise 3: Reflection and Application
1. After completing Exercises 1 and 2, reflect on the process:
   - What challenges did you face in organizing your knowledge?

- How did creating these guides enhance your understanding of the topics?
2. Develop a plan for using personal knowledge guides in your future learning:
    - Identify upcoming topics or areas of study
    - Schedule regular review and update sessions for your guides
3. Share your experience:
    - Discuss your personal knowledge guide with a peer or mentor
    - Gather feedback on the clarity and effectiveness of your guide

Chapter 11: Using the Absorption Framework to Build Your Cognitive System

In our journey of learning, we encounter countless experiences, both big and small. These experiences yield not only knowledge itself but also a precious skill—the ability to "absorb." This absorption is the process of establishing connections between new knowledge and our existing understanding, weaving a tapestry of interconnected ideas.

When we build a knowledge system in a subject area, we're essentially creating a framework composed of a trunk and main branches. This structure provides a place for additional knowledge to "attach" itself, transforming disparate pieces of information into a cohesive whole.

The process of learning any topic follows a similar pattern. We begin with a problem to solve, gathering information and knowledge along the way. We adopt a knowledge outline that suits our needs, then continue to learn and master more knowledge and skills. Through practice, we become proficient and gradually expand our understanding. Finally, we create opportunities to teach what we've learned to others. As we cycle through this process repeatedly, our understanding of the subject area deepens exponentially.

Throughout this journey, various pieces of knowledge are absorbed and attached to our knowledge outline. As our learning progresses, the outline we initially borrowed from elsewhere undergoes significant changes. We make modifications to suit our unique needs, create new connections between knowledge points, and transform it into our own distinctive knowledge framework. This process of transformation and integration is what we call the "absorption framework."

The Absorption Framework: A Cycle of Growth

The absorption framework can be distilled into four key stages: Learning, Verification, Expansion, and Results. This framework is versatile, applying equally well to three types of learning: knowledge acquisition, tool mastery, and skill development. It can be used for internal cycles of learning within a specific subject area, as well as external cycles that incorporate related knowledge from outside the primary field of study.

Let's examine how this framework operates in both internal and external cycles:

Internal Cycle

1. Learning: This stage refers to the focused acquisition of knowledge within the subject area. The penetration learning method suggests starting by adopting a high-quality knowledge outline from an external source. Then, using methods like deep replication in five steps and sprint reading, we build a solid foundation of knowledge.
2. Verification: As we learn, we continuously test ourselves on the knowledge points we've acquired. This self-assessment helps us verify our level of mastery. When learning tools or skills, we gauge our real level of proficiency through practical application.
3. Expansion: After verification, we further expand and deepen our understanding of the verified knowledge points. For tools and skills, this step involves continuous practice,

achieving proficiency, and applying our knowledge in practical situations. Through this process, we expand our knowledge reserve.

4. Results: This final stage involves displaying our learning outcomes or demonstrating the effectiveness of our knowledge in practical applications. It corresponds to the explaining step in the Feynman Technique, where we solidify our understanding by teaching others.

These results are not the end of the journey, but merely a step in the cycle. After we achieve results with one part of our knowledge, we return to the learning stage to continue with the next knowledge point, perpetuating the cycle of growth.

External Cycle

1. Learning: In the broader context, this stage refers to establishing our overall knowledge system in the subject area. We create a comprehensive framework that integrates various aspects of our field of study.
2. Verification: We put the knowledge we've learned to the test in real-world situations.

We retain the knowledge proven effective and transform some application methods into our own unique approaches.
3. Expansion: At this stage, we meticulously sort out the knowledge we've acquired, expanding and deepening key parts. Writing a personal knowledge guide plays a crucial role here. We add our own new ideas and establish novel connections between existing knowledge points, thereby expanding our knowledge system.
4. Results: The culmination of the external cycle involves teaching this entire system to others. Through this process of sharing and explaining, we achieve a sublimation of our own cognitive level, reinforcing and elevating our understanding.

By employing the absorption framework in both internal and external cycles, we create a dynamic and ever-evolving cognitive system. This system not only enhances our personal understanding but also positions us to make meaningful contributions to our field of study. As we continue to absorb, integrate, and share knowledge, we embark on a lifelong journey of learning and growth.

Transforming External Knowledge into Personal Expertise

Techniques for Knowledge Absorption

1. Active Engagement with Material:
    - Mark, excerpt, take notes, write summaries, and copy outlines
    - Organize excerpts and notes into structured lists
    - Redraw diagrams from learning materials
    - Apply the Feynman Technique: Explain concepts to others to identify gaps in understanding
2. Personalization of Learning:
    - Use tools to create your own customized textbook
    - Follow practical examples in learning materials to gain hands-on experience
    - Modify learned methods to fit your specific situation and document these adaptations
    - Write a personal knowledge guide to summarize and organize learned information

3. Application and Value Creation:
   - Put learned concepts into practice and document results
   - Transform learning outcomes into valuable products or services for others

Practical Techniques for the Absorption Framework

1. Mind Mapping:
   - Organize knowledge into hierarchical outlines (max 4 levels)
   - Use minimalist format: central topic, branch topics, subtopics
   - Adjust relationships by dragging items
   - Utilize various viewing options for different perspectives
2. Bullet-Point Lists:
   - Employ for note-taking and drafting
   - Use three types: simple checklist, explanatory list, multi-level list
3. One-Page Magic:
   - Compress information onto a single A4 page
   - Ensure content is easily readable at a glance

4. Diagramming Knowledge:
    - Create visual representations of processes and relationships
    - Continuously iterate and improve diagrams
5. Writing for Comprehension:
    - Document expected outcomes and compare with actual results
    - Record explanations when using the Feynman Technique
    - Publish notes online for public practice
    - Rephrase new information in your own words
6. Teaching to Others:
    - Prepare a lecture outline in list form
    - Use outline during explanation and for post-teaching reflection
7. Identifying Personal Learning Style:
    - Reflect on how you best absorb and transmit information
    - Consider your preferred learning tools and methods

Key Points of This Chapter

- The "absorption framework" consists of four cyclical steps: Learning, Verification, Expansion, and Results
- Seven key techniques support the absorption framework:
    1. Mind mapping
    2. Bullet-point listing
    3. One-page summarization
    4. Diagramming
    5. Writing for comprehension
    6. Teaching others
    7. Identifying personal learning style

Practical Exercises
1. Personalized Learning Techniques:
    - Review the list of techniques provided in this chapter
    - Add your own unique methods to the end of the list
    - Reflect on which techniques have been most effective for you
2. Learning Reflection and Future Planning:
    - Create two lists:
    a. Concepts from this book you've successfully internalized
    b. Topics you plan to master in the coming year

- Share these lists with a learning partner or mentor for feedback and accountability
3. Absorption Framework Implementation:
    - Choose a new topic of interest
    - Apply the four-step absorption framework to this topic
    - Document your progress through each stage
    - Reflect on how the framework enhanced your learning process
4. Teaching Challenge:
    - Select a concept from this book that you feel you've mastered
    - Prepare a short lesson (5-10 minutes) to teach this concept
    - Deliver the lesson to a friend or family member
    - Gather feedback and reflect on areas for improvement
5. Mind Map Creation:
    - Develop a comprehensive mind map of the key concepts in this book
    - Limit your map to four levels of hierarchy

- Share your mind map with fellow learners for comparison and discussion

Afterword: Everyone Can Become a Learning Expert

As we conclude this exploration of learning, it's important to reflect on the journey we've taken together. This book serves as a guide to enhancing your learning capabilities and addresses three fundamental questions:

1. How can we effectively engage with the current technological revolution through learning?
2. How can we utilize new technological tools to significantly improve our learning and work efficiency?
3. How can we reduce our learning time to a fraction of what it once was?

The answers to these questions lie in the consistent application of the Feynman learning method, which has been emphasized throughout this book. By integrating this method with AI tools, you can achieve not only improvements in efficiency but also meaningful innovations and breakthroughs.

Our hope is that this book provides valuable guidance for those who may feel passive in their learning journey, empowers active learners to thrive, and inspires anyone who wishes to reignite their enthusiasm for learning.

We find ourselves in an era rich with opportunities for personal growth. With the right mindset and resources, anyone can become a proficient learner. The process of learning can be engaging, and AI can assist you in discovering your preferred learning style and methods.

Thank you for taking the time to read this book. Your commitment to enhancing your learning skills is commendable. If you found value in this work, we would appreciate it if you could leave a review. Your feedback is invaluable and helps others consider embarking on their own journey of enhanced learning.

References

Ackoff, R. L. (1989). From data to wisdom. Journal of Applied Systems Analysis, 16(1), 3-9.

Ahrens, S. (2017). How to take smart notes: One simple technique to boost writing, learning and thinking. CreateSpace Independent Publishing Platform.

Allen, D. (2015). Getting things done: The art of stress-free productivity (Revised ed.). Penguin Books.

Browne, M. N., & Keeley, S. M. (2007). Asking the right questions: A guide to critical thinking (8th ed.). Pearson.

Ericsson, K. A., & Pool, R. (2016). Peak: Secrets from the new science of expertise. Houghton Mifflin Harcourt.

Forte, T. (2022). Building a second brain: A proven method to organize your digital life and unlock your creative potential. Atria Books.

Gabriele, M. (2023, June 25). AI and the burden of knowledge. The Generalist. https://www.generalist.com/briefing/ai-and-the-burden-of-knowledge

Gladwell, M. (2008). Outliers: The story of success. Little, Brown and Company.

Gleick, J. (1992). Genius: The life and science of Richard Feynman. Pantheon Books.

Jones, B. F. (2009). The burden of knowledge and the "death of the renaissance man": Is innovation getting harder? The Review of Economic Studies, 76(1), 283-317.

Klement, A. (2018). When coffee and kale compete: Become great at making products people will buy. NYC Press.

LeCun, Y., Bengio, Y., & Hinton, G. (2015). Deep learning. Nature, 521(7553), 436-444. https://www.nature.com/articles/nature14539

Luhmann, N. (1992). Communicating with slip boxes: An empirical account. In A. Kieserling

(Ed.), Universität als Milieu: Kleine Schriften (pp. 53-61). Haux.

Moore, B. N., & Parker, R. (2011). Critical thinking (10th ed.). McGraw-Hill Education.

Newport, C. (2016). Deep work: Rules for focused success in a distracted world. Grand Central Publishing.

Silver, D., Huang, A., Maddison, C. J., Guez, A., Sifre, L., van den Driessche, G., Schrittwieser, J., Antonoglou, I., Panneershelvam, V., Lanctot, M., Dieleman, S., Grewe, D., Nham, J., Kalchbrenner, N., Sutskever, I., Lillicrap, T., Leach, M., Kavukcuoglu, K., Graepel, T., & Hassabis, D. (2016). Mastering the game of Go with deep neural networks and tree search. Nature, 529(7587), 484-489. https://www.nature.com/articles/nature16961

Statista. (2023). Number of ChatGPT users worldwide from December 2022 to January 2023.

Turing, A. M. (1950). Computing machinery and intelligence. Mind, 59(236), 433-460. https://

academic.oup.com/mind/article/LIX/236/433/986238

Vaswani, A., Shazeer, N., Parmar, N., Uszkoreit, J., Jones, L., Gomez, A. N., Kaiser, Ł., & Polosukhin, I. (2017). Attention is all you need. In Advances in Neural Information Processing Systems (pp. 5998-6008). https://proceedings.neurips.cc/paper/2017/file/3f5ee243547dee91fbd053c1c4a845aa-Paper.pdf

www.ingramcontent.com/pod-product-compliance
Lightning Source LLC
Chambersburg PA
CBHW052205220526
45471CB00004B/1820